I0440887

GOVERNMENT OF YE OLDE NEW ENGLAND,INC

Post Office Box 1111

SAVANNAH, TN 38372

731-727-4537

STEPHENMAXWELLMINISTRIES@YAHOO.COM

WHAT WE ARE ALL ABOUT?

WE ARE AN GOVERNMENT THAT HOLDS TO THE BELIEFS OF BOTH THE GOSPEL OF JESUS CHRIST AND HOW THEY USED TO GOVERN AND LIVE IN THE 17TH TO THE EARLY 20TH CENTURY;WHEN GOVERNMENT WAS GOVERNED BY "WE THE PEOPLE"; NOT BY BIG GOVERNMENT. WE THE PEOPLE VOTE IN THE PRESIDENT, NOT THE CONGRESS OF OUR GOVERNMENT.

WHO ARE WE??

WE ARE A PEOPLE THAT ARE TIRED OF BIG GOVERNMENT. WE ARE TIRED OF PERJURY. WE ARE TIRED OF HIGH TAXES. WE ARE TIRED OF IMPROPER REPRESENTATION. WE ARE NOT BELIEVERS OR TRUST IN THOSE THAT HAVE A PLAN READY TO BE "EXEMPT" FROM GOVERNMENTAL ISSUES OR LAWS THAT THE CONGRESS MAKES LAW. WE ARE A

PEOPLE WHO ARE TRULY CHRISTIAN. WE ARE A PEOPLE THAT ARE READY TO BE SET FREE FROM TYRANNY. WE ARE A PEOPLE THAT ARE SICK OF DICTATORSHIP RATHER THAN A TRUE PRESIDENCY.

WHO ARE THE GOVERNMENTS OR LEADERS THAT WE RECOGNIZE AS PEACEFUL GOVERNMENTS EVEN IF WE PUT OBJECTION BY IT?

WE RECOGNIZE THE GOVERNMENT OF THE UNITED STATES OF AMERICA WITH OBJECTION.

WE RECOGNIZED THE GOVERNMENT AND KINGDOM OF ISRAEL.

WE RECOGNIZED THE GOVERNMENT AND KINGDOM OF GREAT BRITAIN, ESPECIALLY HER MAJESTY THE QUEEN AND ALL HER REALMS, ELIZABETH R. II.

WE ARE A NON-PROFIT ORGANIZATION

HOW MUCH DOES A PERSON HAVE TO PAY TO BE IN THE GOVERNMENT???
WE ASK FOR $100.00 DUES TO BE IN THE GOVERNMENT; THESE ARE NOT TAXES; THIS IS SO THAT WE CAN RUN FROM DAY TO DAY BUSNIESS; WITHOUT WORRYING ABOUT THE DAY TO DAY; MONTH TO MONTH DAILY BILLING SUCH AS LIGHTS; WATER; GAS.

OUR OFFICERS/JUDICIAL COMMITTEE

OUR PRESIDENT- REV. STEPHEN C. MAXWELL, A MAN OF MID 30'S IS A MAN THAT DOES NOT BELIEVE IN HARRASSING; INTIMIDATION OR PROFESSIONAL MISCONDUCT OF ANY PROFESSIONAL IN THE GOVERNMENT. PRESIDENT MAXWELL HAS WITH THE MADAM VICE PRESIDENT AND MR. SPEAKER'S HELP; FOUNDED THIS GOVERNMENT WITH A IDEA AND A VISION THAT THERE WOULD BE A GOVERNMENT THAT WOULD NOT BE TOTALATARIAN; SUCH AS THE ONE WE LIVE IN.

MADAM VICE PRESIDENT-   A PHENOMENAL WOMAN BORN OF THE MID 1900'S; A WOMAN OF GREAT VISION AND DREAMS; THE VICE PRESIDENT DEISRED WITH THE PRESIDENT; THAT THIS GOVERNMENT WOULD BE A PLACE; AN EMBASSY; THAT WOULD BE SEPARATE FROM ANY GOVERNMENT; TO HELP A PEOPLE; BOTH OF HEALTH AND SOCIAL ISSUES. THE VICE PRESIDENT HAS A DESIRE TO BE A MINISTERIAL GUIDE FOR THE LOST SOULS, THUS OUR MOTTO.**MR. SPEAKER-** THE SPEAKER OF THE HOUSE, A MAN OF TRUE VISION AND ONE OF TRUTH, ONE WHO BELIEVES IN REALITY, A DIFFERENT TYPE OF PERSON;ONE WHO HAS WORKED CLOSELY WITH PEOPLE; ONE WHO HAS A HEART FOR PEOPLE; AN INDIVIDUAL WHO BELIEVES IN HARD WORK AND LOOKS DOWN ON LAZINESS; SUCH AS THOSE IN THE GOVERNMENT WE LIVE IN TODAY. MR.

SPEAKER DOES NOT BELIEVE IN ANY SHANNANIGANS THAT ARE GOING ON IN TODAY'S ECONOMY OR THAT OF THE U.S. GOVERNMENT THAT WILL REVOKE ANY PERSON THAT COMES UP AGAINST THEM. MR. SPEAKER HAS A BIG HEART FOR BOTH PEOPLE AND ANIMALS.

Update- There is no more Speaker of the House. Our Vice President is deceased as of March 2016.

CONSTITUTION OF THE GOVERNMENT OF YE OLDE NEW ENGLAND

PREAMBLE- WE THE PEOPLE, PURSUING

THE GOALS OF HIGHER AND BETTER GOVERNMENT AND ALLEGIANCE TO JESUS CHRIST OF NAZARETH SPELLED OUT IN THIS CONSTITUTION; ESTALBISH THIS GOVERNMENT

SECCEEDING FROM THE GOVERNMENT OF THE UNITED STATES; WE DO HOWEVER, RECOGNIZE THE GOVERNMENT OF THE UNITED STATES OF AMERICA AND THEIR REPRESENTATIVES, WE

ARE NOT
ESTABLISHING THIS
GOVERNMENT TO
ESTABLISH TAX
EVASION NOR ANY
CRIMINAL ACTIVITIES;
INCLUDING WAR
CRIMES. WE ORDAIN
THIS CONSTITUTION AS

THE CONSTITUTION OF THE GOVERNMENT OF YE OLDE NEW ENGLAND.

ARTICLE ONE- STATE/PEOPLE (CITIZENSHIP/LANGUAGE)

1. CITIZENS ARE BACKROUND CHECKED WHO SHALL BE KNOWN AS CITIZEN-ELECT UNTIL SWORN IN BY THE PRESIDENT; THE CHILDREN OF OUR CITIZENS SHALL BE AUTOMATICALLY CITIZENS AND SWORN IN @14 YEARS OF AGE.
2. THE LANGUAGE OF THIS GOVERNMENT SHALL BE ENGLISH

ARTICE TWO- STATE SOVERIENGTY

1. THIS STATE IS KJV BIBLICALLY, SOVERIENG AND DEMOCRATIC REPUBLIC. ALL ENTITIES MUST YIELD TO JESUS AND THIS CONSTITUTION.

2. THE BIBLE AND THIS CONSTITUTION IS THE SUPREME LAWS OF THE LAND. THE BIBLE AND CONSTITUTION ARE DIRECTLY BINDING ON ALL STATE AUTHORITY

ARTICLE THREE- NATIONALISM

1. THE STATE HAS NATIONAL COLORS; STATE FLAG; SEAL AND COAT OF ARMS. HEAVENS JUBILEE WILL BE OUR NATIONAL ANTHEM.
2. THE STATE MOTTO IS "HELPING THOSE THAT ARE LOST, FIND THEIR WAY"
3. THE CAPITOL OF THIS STATE SHALL BE SAVANNAH, TN 38372

CHAPTER 2- STATE OBJECTIVES

GENERAL CONSTITUTION OBJECTIVES

1. THE STATE PROMOTES UNIVERSAL JUSTICE AND UNIVERSAL PROTECTION OF HUMAN RIGHTS AS INDIVIDUAL RIGHTS. THE STATE ENCOURAGES FRATERNITY AMONGST ITS CITIZENS MALE TO FEMALE BY ESTABLISHING GENERAL WELFARE AND UNTIY.

2. THE STATE ACKNOWLEDGES THE RIGHT OF THE PEOPLE TO NATIONAL AUTONOMY AND SELF-DETERMINATION AND THE RIGHT OF MINORITIES TO GROUP AUTONOMY.

3. THE STATE PROMOTES:

A. BIBLICAL; MORAL; SPIRITUAL LIFE

B. CHRISTIAN EDUCATION AND SCHOOLING

C. IF AT ALL POSSIBLE ALL CITIZENS TO BE SELF-SUFFICIENT

D. THE MEN AND WOMEN OF THIS STATE SHALL BE EQUAL; WITH THE EXCEPTION THE WOMEN CANNOT BE PRESIDENT OF THIS GOVERNMENT.

E. THOSE THAT CAN TO STUDY BIBLICAL SCIENCE AND THE ARTS

F. SAMLL GOVERNMENT; WE THE PEOPLE ESTABLISH THIS GOVERNMENT BY VOTE AND VOICE AND ALL ARE CONSIDERED IN LEGISLATION

G. ABORTION; ADULTREY; FORNICATION; GAY LIFESTYLES ARE FORBIDDEN AND ILLEGAL.

4. THE SEAL OF AUTHORIZATION SHALL BE THE BROWN GAVEL WITH THE BLACK WORDS OF "LAW" ON IT; THE CHRISTIAN FLAG OPPOSITE OF

THE GAVEL WITH THE WORD "GRACE" ON IT; WITH A BALD EAGLE IN BETWEEN THE TWO OF THEM WITH WINGSPAND LEFT AND RIGHT; THE EAGLE FACING RIGHT WITH THE WORDS IN BLACK "SEAL OF THE CLERGY" UNDERNEATH THE EMBLEM.

5. THE FLAG SHALL BE ONE WITH A CROSS IN THE MIDDLE OF THE FLAG; WITH THE WORDS "GOVERNMENT OF YE OLDE NEW ENGLAND" IN BLACK IN THE MIDDLE OF THE CROSS WITH THE SEAL OF AUTHORIZATION TO ITS RIGHT IN THE UPPER CORNER.

6. OUR COLORS SHALL BE RED; WHITE; BLUE, BROWN AND BLACK W/BLACK LETTERS

7. OUR COAT OF ARMS SHALL BE BLACK AFTER THE NAME OF MAXWELL MEANING "DEEPLY RELIGIOUS"

8. WHEN "HEAVEN'S JUBILEE" IS PLAYED; WE WILL RECOGNIZE IN RESPECT OF ITS AUTHORITY; WE SHALL WORSHIP JESUS IN RESPECT TO THIS SONG IN OVATION AND A WORSHIPFUL SPIRIT.

ARTICLE FIVE – LEGISLATION; EXECUTIVE BRANCHES

1. THE PRESIDENT IS VESTED WITH FULL EXECUTIVE POWER AND AUTHORITY OF THE GOVERNMENT AND THE PEOPLE OF THE STATE FOR THE BENEFIT OF THE GOVERNMENT AND THE PEOPLE OF THE STATE TO OVERTURN/AMEND ALL LAWS
2. THE LEGISLATURE BRANCH SHALL BE MADE UP OF AT LEAST 3 PERSONS AND MAKE/PASS AND SEND ALL BILLS TO THE PRESIDENT. THE PRESIDENT MAY SIGN THE BILL INTO LAW OR VETO IT ON THEIR DISCRETION. ONCE THE BILL IS VETOED; THE BILL IS DEAD.
3. THE HOUSE OF REPRESENTATIVES/SENATE SHALL CONVENE ON THE 10TH OF JANUARY AND START A NEW CONGRESS. SENATORS/REPRESENTATIVES ARE CHARGED TO VOTE 2/3 MAJORITY TO PASS ALL LEGISLATION W/MUCH DEBATE.
4. THE HOUSE AND THE SENATE SHALL ELECT EITHER A SPEAKER OR SENATE PRO TEMPRE; A MAJORITY LEADER; A MINORITY LEADER; WHIP AND A SGT AT ARMS AS OFFICERS IN BOTH HOUSES.

5. BOTH HOUSES MAY COME TO GIVE CONSENT; IF NOT IN SESSION; UNLESS AN OBJECTION IS MADE FOR THE BILL TO PASS TO LAW.

EXECUTIVE BRANCH-

1. THE PRESIDENT WHEN ELECTED SHALL GIVE THE FOLLOWING OATH ON THE 21ST OF JANUARY EVERY YEAR AFTER THIS MANNER:
I_____DO SOLEMNLY AFFIRM THAT I WILL FAITHFULLY EXECUTE THE OFFICE OF THE PRESIDENT OF THE GOVERNMENT OF YE OLDE NEW ENGLAND. THAT I WILL PRESERVE; PROTECT AND DEFEND THE CONSTITUTION AND GOD'S HOLY WORD. SOM HELP ME PLEASE JESUS"

2. THE PRESIDENT SHALL BE THE CIVILIAN COMMANDER IN CHIEF OF ALL ARMED FORCES OF THIS GOVERNMENT

3. THE PRESIDENT FOR THE ESTABLISHMENT OF THIS GOVERNMENT SHALL BE STEPHEN C. MAXWELL UNTIL DEATH; RESIGNATION OR INCAPACITATION

4. THE PRESIDENT CANNOT BE IMPEACHED SAVE FOR THE CAUSE OF ADULTREY OR FORNICATION.

5. THE PRESIDENT SHALL TAKE THE OATH OF OFFICE ON JANUARY 21 OF THE FOLLOWING YEAR ELECTED.
6. CITIZENS MUST BE 14 YEARS OF AGE IN ORDER FOR A BALLOT TO COUNT AGAINST/FOR THE CANDIDATE OF THEIR CHOICE.
7. RIGHTS OF CITIZENS:
   A. RIGHT TO BEAR ARMS
   B. RIGHT TO ATTEND CHURCH OF CHOICE; ESTABLISH CHURCH OF CHOICE; WORSHIP IN CHURCH OF CHOICE; VOICE OVER ANY COMMUNICATION DEVICE OF WORHSIP IN CHURCH OF CHOICE; FREEDOM OF RELIGION WITHOUT OBLIGATION TO THE GOVERNMENT.
   C. RIGHT TO FREEDOM OF THE PRESS
   D. RIGHT TO FREEDOM OF SPEECH
   E. RIGHT TO ASSEMBLE FREELY AND PEACEABLY
   F. RIGHT TO REDRESS GRIEVANCES WITH ANY AND ALL ELECTED OFFICIALS

ARTICLE 7- THE VICE PRESIDENT
1. THE VICE PRESIDENT SHALL COME INTO OFFICE WITH THE PRESIDENT AS CHOSEN.

2. THE VICE PRESIDENT SHALL BE THE HEAD OF THE SENATE. THE VICE PRESIDENT IS CHARGED TO OVERSEE AND BREAK ANY TIES WITHIN THE SENATE FOR THE PASSING/OPPOSITION OF BILLS. THE VICE PRESIDENT SHALL ACCOMPLISH/FULLFILL ANY AND ALL LAWFUL ORDERS/DIRECTIVES GIVEN FROM THE PRESIDENT.

ARTICLE 8-THE PRESIDENTIAL CABINET

THE CABINET SHALL BE APPOINTED AND SWORN IN BY THE PRESIDENT AND ALL CABINET MEMEBERS NEED NOT APPROVAL OF THE LEGISLATURE UNLESS QUESTIONABLE ARRESTS OR INCARCARATIONS ARE ON THEIR RECORD.

THE CABINET SHALL BE MADE UP OF SECRETARIES:

1. POSTMASTER GENERAL
2. SECRETARY OF STATE
3. SECRETARY OF TREASURY
4. AMBASSADOR TO THE U.S.
5. AMBASSADOR TO ISRAEL

6. SECRETARY OF THE INTERIOR
7. SECRETARY OF TRANSPORTATION
8. SECRETARY OF TITHES AND OFFERINGS(SEPARATE FROM TREASURY)

ARTICLE NINE-DISQUALIFICATIONS

THE FOLLOWING DEFENITIONS ARE DISQUALIFICATIONS FROM HOLDING CITIZENSHIP /OFFICE IN OUR GOVERNMENT:

1. NO WOMAN MAY HOLD THE OFFICE OF THE PRESIDENT
2. POOR BACKROUND/CRIMINAL CHECKS
3. NO DOMESTIC ABUSER/SEXUAL OFFENDER/DRUG OFFENDERS
4. NO ONE OF THE ALTERNATIVE LIFESTYLES

ARTICLE 10-PENTECOSTAL CHURCH

THE GOVERNMENT OF YE OLDE NEW ENGLAND SHALL HAVE SERVICES FREELY TO ONE AND ALL ON A NON DENOMINATIONAL BASIS. THESE SERVICES SHALL BE 11AM AND 3PM M-F. THERE SHALL BE AN EVENING SERVICE ON SUNDAY @7PM; IT WILL BE A

PENTECOSTAL WORSHIP ATMOSPHERE. ONLY CLERGY OF THE PENTECOSTAL FAITH SHALL BE RECOGNIZED TO OUR PULPIT; HOWEVER.

ARTICLE 11- THE JUDICIAL BRANCH SHALL BE MADE UP OF 9 JUSTICES; ONE SHALL BE A CHIEF JUSTICE; THE OTHER SHALL BE 8 ASSOCIATE JUSTICES.

1. THE GOVERNMENT'S SUPREME COURT SHALL RULE ACCORDING TO THIS CONSTITUTION AND THE BIBLE AND MAKE THEIR DECISIONS PLAINLY EITHER BY DISIDENTS OR FAVOR.

ARTICLE 12- THE ENFORCEMENT OF THE EXECUTIVE BRANCH

1. THE PRESIDENT SHALL BE PASTOR OF THE GOVERNING CHURCH
2. THE PRESIDENT SHALL BE THE CHIEF EXECUTIVE OFFICER
3. THE PRESIDENT SHALL BE THE COMMANDER IN CHIEF OF ALL ARMED FORCES

4. *THE PRESIDENT MAY DECLARE WAR OR POLICE ACTION WITHOUT PRIOR CONSENT; IF LEGISLATURE IS NOT IN SESSION.*
5. *THE PRESIDENT; LEGISLATURE AND JUDICIAL BRANCHES SHALL BE COMPENSATED ONCE THE GOVERNMENT'S ASSETS REACH OVER $100,000.00 (ONE HUNDRED THOUSAND U.S. DOLLARS)*
6. *THE PRESIDENT MAY MAKE ANY EXECUTIVE ORDER NEEDED OR OPINIONED TO MAKE; AS*

NECESSARY.

THE CONSTITUTIONAL AMENDMENTS-
AMENDMENT ONE-   THE GOVERNMENT; CONGRESS; JUDICIAL; EXECUTIVE BRANCHES OF THIS MICRONATION SHALL IN NO WAY ABRIDGE THE RIGHT TO FREEDOM OF RELIGION IN ALL ASPECTS; NOR THE RIGHT TO WORSHIP; NOR THE RIGHT TO ATTEND THE CHURCH OF ONE'S OWN CHOICE; NOR THE RIGHT TO PREACH ACTS 2:38 AND HEAVEN AND HELL. THE GOVERNMENT BODIES

NAMED THEREIN WITH THE ARMED FORCES SHALL NEVER BE ABLE TO OVERTHROW SAID GOVERNMENT IN ACTS OF TREASON; NEITHER SHALL MARTIAL LAW BE CALLED TO OVERTHROW OUR RIGHTS AS CITIZENS; SAID GOVERNMENT AND BODIES THEREIN SHALL NEVER ABRIDGE THE RIGHT TO FREEDOM OF SPEECH; THE PRESS; PEACEABLE ASSEMBLY; NOR ABRIDGE THE RIGHT TO REDRESS GRIEVANCES TO THE PUBLIC OFFICIALS OR ELECTED.

AMENDMENT TWO- NO ELECTED OFFICIAL; LAW ENFORCEMENT; NOR THE ARMED FORCES SHALL TAKE AWAY THE RIGHT TO BEAR ARMS FROM OUR PRIVATE CONSTITUENTS; NOR PUBLIC OFFICIALS THAT HAVE REACHED THE AGE OF ACCOUNTABLITY; THIS WOULD BE 14 YEARS OF AGE IN THIS GOVERNMENT AND BODY; NOR SHALL THE ARMED FORCES HARBOR THEMSELVES WITHIN PRIVATE HOUSING WITHOUT PROPER PAYMENT DURING PEACE/WAR.

AMENDMENT THREE- AT THE TIME OF PEACE AND NO REQUESTS OF EITHER THE POTUS OR ISRAEL

SHALL THE ADULT MALES BE REQUIRED TO ATTEND INDUCTION TO OUR ARMED FORCES OF THOSE 14-17 YEARS OF AGE.

<u>AMENDMENT FOUR</u>- NO LAW ENFORCEMENT; ARMED FORCES NOR MAGISTRATES OF ANY COURT SHALL BE ALLOWED TO ENTER ANY PREMEIS WITHOUT A WARRANT OF ARREST/SEARCH OR SEIZURE REQUIRING THE OFFICER/MAGISTRATE TO TAKE AN OATH AND NAMING SAID PERSON OR THINGS THEREIN OF THE WARRANT AND WHAT PREMESIS SHALL BE ENTERED FOR THE PURPOSES OF COLLECTING EVIDENCE OF A CRIME OR SUSPECT OF A CRIME. NO PRIVATE CITIZEN/PUBLIC OFFICAIL SHALL BE QUESTIONED WITHOUT A LAWYER PRESENT; NOR SHALL ANY COMMENTS; "CONFESSIONS"; STATEMENTS BE ALLOWED TO BE USED IN THE COURTS OF LAW WITHOUT BOTH DEFENSE AND PROSECUTION AND A JUDGE PRESENT; NOR DOES THE ABOVE SAID PERSONS HAVE TO TAKE THE WITNESS STAND TO TESTIFY AGAINST THEMSELVES.

AMENDMENT FIVE- NO PRIVATE CITIZENS/PUBLIC OFFICIAL SHALL BE VERBALLY THREATENED; OR IMPRISONED FOR NOT MAKING A STATEMENT AGAINST THEMSELVES BEFORE LAW ENFORCEMENT OR COURTS OF LAW.

AMENDMENT SIX- ALL ELECT THAT DESIRE TO BE CITIZENS OF THIS GOVERNMENT SHALL HAVE TO GO THOROUGH BACKROUND CHECKS; AND NO PERSON SHALL BE DISCRIMINATED AGAINST BECAUSE OF RACE; COLOR; CREED NOR HANDICAP. THE ELECT CANNOT HAVE PARTAKEN OF THE ALTERNATIVE LIFESTYLE.

AMENDMENT SEVEN- OUR MAIN LAW OF THE LAND SHALL BE THE HOLY WORD OF GOD; THE TEN COMMANDMENTS; AND THE NEW TESTAMENT OF THE KJV HOLY BIBLE. WE MAINTAIN JESUS CHRIST AS THE HEAD OF LAW OF LAND. ANY VIOLATION OR DEVIATION FROM SAID COMMANDMENTS FOR PURPOSE OF EVASION OR MENTAL RESERVATION THEREIN SHALL BE PROSECUTED TO THE FULLEST EXTENT OF THE LAW.

AMENDMENT EIGHT- LAWSUITS MORE THAN TWENTY DOLLARS (UNITED STATES DOLLARS) SHALL BE HEARD BEFORE A JUDGE AND JURY. THE JURY SHALL HAVE THE FINAL SAY OF HOW MUCH A PLANTIFF SHALL RECEIVE IN MONETARY ISSUANCE.

AMENDMENT NINE- NO BAIL SHALL BE SET FOR THOSE DOCKETS OLDER THAN 30 DAYS; FREEDOM MUST BE GIVEN BACK TO THE SUSPECT AND CRIMINAL RECORDS MUST BE EXPUNGED.

AMENDMENT TEN- THE RIGHTS OF CITIZENS NOT MENTIONED/DELEGATED BY THE SAID GOVERNMENT IS RESERVED TO THE CITIZENS RESPECTIVELY.

AMENDMENT ELEVEN- NO CITIZEN SHALL TAKE UP ARMS OR LAWSUIT AGAINST OTHER MICRONATIONS; NATIONS; NOR OTHER CITIZENS OR PUBLIC OFFICIALS UNTIL SUCH SHALL DO THE SAME AGAINST THE OTHER.

AMENDMENT 12- ONLY CITIZENS SHALL VOTE IN THE PRESIDENT. THE LEGISLATIVE BRANCH WILL VERIFY THE COUNT ON THE VOTES; IS ALL.

AMENDMENT 13- UNLESS FOR PUNISHMENT UNDER PUNITIVE DAMAGES SET BY LAW UNDER A JUDICIAL ORDER; NO PERSON SHALL BE SUBJECT TO SERVITUDE WITHOUT JUST COMPENSATION.

AMENDMENT 14- NO PARENT, GRANDPARENT, GREAT-GRANDPARENT; NOR GREAT-GREAT GRANDPARENT ARE ALLOWED TO GIVE CONSENT FOR WHAT IS ILLEGAL TO DO IN OUR GOVERNMENT; ABORTION OF A FETUS OR BORN BABE

AMENDMENT 15- AT THE BEGINNING OF EACH RESPECTIVE NEW YEAR; ALL CITIZENS SHALL BE REQUIRED TO PAY 100.00 U.S. DOLLARS AND THE QUARTERS OF THE YEAR FOLLOWING.
(MAY; SEPTEMBER)

AMENDMENT 16- NO CITIZEN SHALL ABUSE THEIR BODY IN ANY WAY; SHAPE; FORM; NOR FASHION ESEPCIALLY THROUGH TATTOOING; PIERCING OF THE BODY; TOBACCO; ALCOHOL NOR ILLEGAL DRUGS.

AMENDMENT 17- THERE SHALL BE NO TERM FOR ANY OFFICE. LIFETIME APPOINTMENTS ARE CONFERRED ON ALL TILL DEATH; RESIGNATION; INCAPACITATION; OR TERMINATION BY THE PRESIDENT.

THE PRESIDENT; THE VICE PRESIDENT; PRESIDENTIAL CABINET; LEGISLATIVE BODY AND THE JUDICIAL BRANCH.

THE VICE PRESIDENT IF ONLY A MALE SHALL TAKE THE OFFICE OF PRESIDENT IF THE PRESIDENT CANNOT SERVE FOR REASONS IN THIS AMENDMENT.
THE LINE OF SUCCESSION SHALL BE THE FOLLOWING:
1. POSTMASTER GENERAL

2. SECREATRY OF STATE

3. SECRETARY OF TREASURY

4. AMBASSADOR TO THE UNITED STATES

5. AMBASSADOR TO ISRAEL

6. SECRETARY OF INTERIOR

7. SECREATRY OF TITHES AND OFFERINGS

8. THE LINE OF TOP AUTHORITY IN LEGISLATURE

AMENDMENT EIGHTEEN- THE RIGHT TO VOTE
SHALL NOT BE ABRIGED FOR LACK OF POLL TAX OR
PAYMENT; NEITHER IF THE VOTER IS 14; BUT ONLY
IF THE 100.00 FUNDS HAVE NOT BEEN UP TO DATE
IN DUES.

WRITTEN IN THE YEAR 2011
REVISED IN THE YEAR OF 2013/3/31
CORRECTED AND REVISED IN THE YEAR OF
2013/4/25 FOR GRAMMATICAL ERRORS
FOUND.(SM)
PRESIDENT-THE HONORABLE REV. STEPHEN C.
MAXWELL
VICE PRESIDENT-THE HONORABLE REV. CRYSTAL J.
FIGUEROA

SPEAKER OF THE HOUSE OF REPRESENTATIVES- THE HONORABLE MIGUEL A. FIGUEROA

GOVERNMENT OF YE OLDE NEW ENGLAND, INC.

55 BOBBY LANE

SAVANNAH, TN 38372

(731)-412-8961

(731)-727-6812

YOU HOLD US UNRESPONSIBLE FOR ANY UNFORSEEN PROBLEMS.

THANK YOU FOR YOUR INTEREST IN JOINING OUR GOVERNMENT. PLEASE FILL OUT THE INFORMATION BELOW. PLEASE GET THIS APPLICATION AND THE $100.00 NON-REFUNDABLE DUES BACK TO US. YOU ARE INFORMED; DUES ARE DUE AT THE $100.00 INCRAMENT FROM MAY 1 TO MAY 31ST OF THE SAME YEAR AND SEPTEMBER 1ST TO SEMTEMBER 30TH OF THE SAME YEAR. EVERY JANUARY OF THE RESPECTIVE YEAR; _EVERYONE IS TO PAY THEIR DUES; PLEASE!_

The Following is _MANDATORY TO SIGN!_

I solemnly affirm that I will support and defend the Constitution of Government of Ye Olde New England; against all enemies foreign and domestic; that I take this Obligation freely; without mental reservation or purpose of evasion; and that I will well and faithfully discharge the duties of the office that I am about to enter. SO HELP ME LORD JESUS!

The Office I want to apply for:

1. Citizen
2. Senator
3. Representative
4. Presidential Cabinet as Secretary/Other

THERE IS A NON-REFUNDABLE $100.00 DUE EVERY JANUARY; MAY AND SEPTEMBER.

PRINT _____   DATE _____

SIGN _____ DATE _____

ALL VOTES SENT THROUGH THE UNITED STATES POSTAL SERVICE:
MUST BE SENT CERTIFIED MAIL AND YOUR VOTE MUST BE SIGNED BY A NOTARY PUBLIC;
PLEASE!

PRINT NAME_____DATE_____

SIGN NAME_____DATE_____

GOVERNMENT OF YE OLDE NEW ENGLAND, INC.

55 BOBBY LANE

SAVANNAH, TN 38372

(731)-412-8961

(731)-727-6812

PLEASE TELL US ABOUT YOURSELF…….

NAME_____

ADDRESS_____

CITY_____STATE_____ZIP_____

PHONE (DAYTIME)_____ CELL_____

EMAIL(OPTIONAL)_____

HAVE YOU EVER WORKED FOR A NON-PROFIT BEFORE??

ARE YOU CHRISTIAN/DO YOU CLAIM TO BE? /DO YOU WANT TO BE?

CAN YOU SIT BEFORE A COMMITTEE AND SPEAK THE TRUTH????

WOULD YOU HAVE A PROBLEM SITTING BEFORE US AS A COMMITTEE, IN AN INTERVIEW AND INVESTIGATION????

THANK YOU FOR YOUR TIME.

STATE OF _____

COUNTY OF_____

NOW COMES BEFORE ME, ONE,_____ WHO HAS
GIVEN THE ABOVE STATEMENT UNDER OATH UNDER THAT STATE AND FEDERAL LAWS OF PERJURY
AND SOLEMNLY AFFIRMS THAT THE ABOVE STATEMENT IS TRUE AND CORRECT TO THE BEST OF
_____ KNOWLEDGE ON THIS_____DAY OF_____,20_____.

SIGNATURE CF AFFIANT_____

DATE_____

NOTARY SIGNATURE_____DATE:_____ **(SEAL)**

PLEASE TEAR OUT, FILL OUT AND SEND, THANK YOU! THIS IS ONLY IF YOU'RE INTERESTED; SERIOUS INQUIRIES ONLY AND ONLY IF YOU CAN PAY THE DUES. (SM)

www.ingramcontent.com/pod-product-compliance
Lightning Source LLC
Chambersburg PA
CBHW071346310526
45790CB00018B/1374